FALLEN ANGELS

Walter Dean Myers

TECHNICAL DIRECTOR Maxwell Krohn
EDITORIAL DIRECTOR Justin Kestler
MANAGING EDITOR Ben Florman

SERIES EDITORS Boomie Aglietti, Justin Kestler
PRODUCTION Christian Lorentzen

WRITERS Yael Goldstein, Selena Ward
EDITORS Matt Blanchard, Karen Schrier

This edition published by Spark Publishing

Spark Publishing
A Division of SparkNotes LLC
120 Fifth Avenue, 8th Floor
New York, NY 10011

02 03 04 05 SN 9 8 7 6 5 4 3 2 1

Please send all comments and questions or report errors to
feedback@sparknotes.com.

Library of Congress information available upon request

Printed and bound in the United States

RRD-C

ISBN 1-58663-512-3

INTRODUCTION: STOPPING TO BUY SPARKNOTES ON A SNOWY EVENING

Whose words these are you *think* you know.
Your paper's due tomorrow, though;
We're glad to see you stopping here
To get some help before you go.

Lost your course? You'll find it here.
Face tests and essays without fear.
Between the words, good grades at stake:
Get great results throughout the year.

Once school bells caused your heart to quake
As teachers circled each mistake.
Use SparkNotes and no longer weep,
Ace every single test you take.

Yes, books are lovely, dark, and deep,
But only what you grasp you keep,
With hours to go before you sleep,
With hours to go before you sleep.

CONTENTS

NOTE: This SparkNote refers to the Scholastic edition of *Fallen Angels*, which does not include numbered chapters. For ease of reference, this SparkNote numbers the sections of the novel.

CONTEXT

WALTER DEAN MYERS WAS BORN in West Virginia in 1937. Myers's mother died three years after his birth, and his father, too poor to raise him, put him into foster care. His foster parents lived in the African-American neighborhood of Harlem in New York City, and he spent most of his childhood and young adulthood there. Though Myers describes his young life as happy—filled with basketball games, a loving upbringing, and good books—he suffered from a speech impediment that made it difficult for him to communicate with others, and at first filled him with rage. Unable to reach out verbally, Myers turned to writing, pouring out his thoughts in poems and short stories. He spent hours in the public library, reading anything he could get his hands on. By the time Myers reached high school, he knew he had intellectual potential, but also knew that his family was too poor to send him to college. Discouraged, he dropped out of school at age fifteen, and though he was persuaded to return, he dropped out again at sixteen. In 1954, on his seventeenth birthday, he joined the army.

Upon his release from the army, Myers had few job skills and little education, and he still suffered from his speech impediment. He took a job loading trucks and then worked in a number of odd jobs in places such as the New York State Department of Labor, a post office, and a rehabilitation center. Myers also kept writing throughout this time, submitting his work to various magazines and periodicals. In 1969, Myers's career received a boost when his novel *Where Does a Day Go?* won a contest sponsored by the Council on Interracial Books for Children. Since then, Myers has been able to support himself with his writing, turning out a large number of books for children and young adults. Two of Myers's novels have won the Newbery Honor Award, and five, including *Fallen Angels,* have earned him the Coretta Scott King Award. In addition to prose fiction, Myers has written poetry and nonfiction work for young adults. In 1984, more than two decades after leaving high school, he graduated from Empire State College. He currently lives in Jersey City, New Jersey, where he writes full time and volunteers in local schools.

Myers has drawn heavily from his own life experiences in writing his novels. He has frequently written about basketball, one of his favorite pastimes, and has set many of his works in his familiar childhood neighborhood of Harlem. Like Richie Perry in *Fallen Angels,* Myers joined the army as a teenager. Despite this frequent reliance on his own experience, however, Myers has also incorporated a number of historical and foreign settings in his novels. *Fallen Angels* takes place in Vietnam, a theater of war in which Myers never served since he was in the army too early.

The Vietnam War lasted from 1959 to 1973. The United States reached its highest level of involvement in the war in approximately 1967, the year in which *Fallen Angels* is set. The conflict arose from American fears that the Communist regime in North Vietnam might conquer the southern part of the country, unifying the two halves under Communist leadership. Though many saw the Vietnam War as essentially a civil war and believed the United States should not have become involved, the United States government believed intervention was necessary to stop the spread of Communism. This idea was called the domino theory, since it focused on the possibility that if South Vietnam fell under Communist control, all of Southeast Asia would follow, in effect setting off a Communist chain reaction throughout many countries. The Americans assisted the South Vietnamese with military advice, modern weapons technology, massive bombing campaigns, and combat troops, which at first seemed successful in pushing back the Communist forces. However, the guerilla tactics of the North Vietnamese proved surprisingly resilient to modern American methods of warfare, and the United States pulled out of Vietnam in 1973, failing to accomplish its goal. Saigon, the capital of South Vietnam, fell to Communist rule in 1975.

Plot Overview

U NCERTAIN OF HIS FUTURE GOALS, seventeen-year-old Richie Perry, a black high school graduate from Harlem, travels to Vietnam to fight in the United States Army. When Richie leaves basic training for Vietnam, he harbors a host of illusions about the war and the army. He confidently believes that the medical profile he has received for a knee injury will be properly processed and prevent him from engaging in combat. He also believes in the flurry of rumors about imminent peace and in the prevalent romantic myths about warfare.

When Richie first arrives in Vietnam, he befriends Harold "Peewee" Gates and Jenkins, two new recruits assigned to the same squad. A sergeant assures them that they should encounter only easy, light work, as there is not much fighting near Chu Lai, where their company is stationed. These rumors prove to be wishful thinking, however, when the three new soldiers arrive at their camp; Jenkins is killed by a land mine during the squad's first patrol. Richie is deeply shaken and longs to communicate his terror and horror to his family, but he finds himself unable to write the truth to his mother and his brother, Kenny.

As Richie witnesses ever-increasing levels of destruction and brutality, he begins to doubt whether there is any straightforward morality in war. He sees that the line between good and bad is often ambiguous. He also becomes disillusioned with the selfishness of his commanding officers, particularly the company commander, Captain Stewart, who is more concerned with earning a promotion than he is with the safety of the soldiers under his command. When Richie's platoon leader, Lieutenant Carroll, is killed during a combat mission, Richie begins a serious search for answers to why he and his fellow soldiers are even fighting in Vietnam in the first place. Though his friends insist that such thoughts are futile and dangerous, Richie feels compelled to find meaning within the chaos. He also longs for some way to communicate his confused thoughts and emotions to his family, but he remains unable to do so. Richie is not sure how to sort out the emotions he feels or how to communicate them effectively to civilians who have never seen combat.

As Richie searches for meaning in the war, he also searches for his own sense of self. He struggles to unravel his motivations for enlisting in the army, wondering whether his reason was a selfless one, based on the desire to earn money to provide for Kenny, or a selfish one—simply to escape from the hard life he faced in Harlem. Richie also forces himself to confront the uncomfortable question of what he will do when he returns to civilian life. Though he is highly intelligent and highly motivated and has ambitions to become a writer, his family is too poor to send him to college. Richie's father abandoned the family years ago, and his mother has since become an alcoholic. Richie is afraid that without an education he has no career potential, and he is unsure what he has to look forward to if he survives.

Richie is wounded in a battle and transferred to a hospital. During the peaceful weeks spent recuperating, he begins to remember the joys of safety and gains a new sense of the horrors of war. When he is declared healthy and ordered to rejoin his unit, he wonders how he can possibly go back into combat and considers deserting the army. In the end, though, he rejoins his unit as ordered.

Back with his unit, Richie learns that the old squad leader, Sergeant Simpson, has been sent home. His replacement is the racist Sergeant Dongan, who always places black soldiers in the most dangerous positions. Early in their tour of duty, there are racial and ethnic tensions among the squad members, which frequently result in physical confrontations. As the squad's bond grows stronger, however, petty prejudices begin to fade, and the squad bands together against Dongan's racism. Soon, Dongan is killed, and the squad is placed under the command of one of its own soldiers, Corporal Brunner.

Brunner leads the men on a deadly mission to track down a group of Vietcong—North Vietnamese guerilla forces—along a river. After a series of mistakes and miscalculations, a firefight breaks out, leaving both Richie and Peewee wounded. Richie's medical profile is finally processed while he is recovering, and Peewee's wounds are serious enough to earn him a discharge from the army. Peewee and Richie fly home on the same plane, along with caskets containing dead soldiers. They try to stand tall for the new recruits, who are just arriving in Vietnam.

Character List

Richie Perry The narrator and protagonist. Richie is a seventeen-year-old high school graduate from Harlem. Though he is smart and ambitious, his alcoholic single mother cannot afford to send him to college, so he joins the army to escape an uncertain future. Richie is sent to Vietnam, and during his months there, he suffers numerous harrowing combat experiences and tries to grapple with the meaning of war, heroism, and good and evil.

Kenny Richie's younger brother. Kenny depends on his older brother, who acts as a father figure to him and enlists in Vietnam in part to help support him. Yet Richie seems to need Kenny just as much as Kenny needs him. Kenny's dependence on Richie and his admiration and love for him act as Richie's only solid link to the civilian world during the war and provide him with his only sense of purpose.

Mother Richie's mother, a depressive alcoholic who has barely functioned since her husband left her years earlier. Though Richie and his mother have never gotten along well, they realize how much they need each other while Richie is in Vietnam. They try to repair their damaged relationship through their letters.

Harold "Peewee" Gates Richie's closest friend in Vietnam. Peewee copes with the fear and uncertainty of the war with comical bravado, though he occasionally allows his true emotions to peek through the bluster.

Lobel   A member of Richie's squad. Jewish and possibly homosexual, Lobel is the target of prejudice nearly as frequently as the black soldiers, to whom he pledges his support in racial skirmishes. Lobel is a devoted fan of the movies, and he distances himself from the horror of battle by imagining that he is merely playing a role in a war film.

Monaco   A soldier of Italian descent on Richie's squad. Monaco seems slightly braver than the rest, always taking the dangerous position of point man.

Captain Stewart   The commander of Richie's company. Captain Stewart wants to be promoted to major, but his company needs to accrue a higher enemy body count for him to earn the promotion. He sends Richie's company on numerous dangerous missions, risking the lives of the soldiers under his command for the sake of his own ambition.

Sergeant Simpson   The leader of Richie's squad. When Richie first arrives in Vietnam, Sergeant Simpson is near the end of his tour of duty. He warns Richie and the other new soldiers not to get him killed because of their inexperience. Later, under great pressure from Stewart, Simpson extends his tour by thirty days, but he survives and returns home, just as he wished.

Lieutenant Carroll   The leader of Richie's platoon. A smart and sympathetic leader, Lieutenant Carroll is well-liked by the men under his command, and his death during combat leaves them all grief-stricken.

Lieutenant Gearhart   The inexperienced leader of Richie's platoon after Lieutenant Carroll's death.

Brew   A devoutly religious solider in Richie's squad. Brew plans to join the ministry upon his return to civilian life.

Corporal Brunner An ambitious soldier on Richie's squad. A bully, Corporal Brunner constantly kisses up to soldiers of higher rank, while abusing those below him.

Sergeant Dongan An officer who replaces Simpson as the leader of Richie's squad. Sergeant Dongan is a racist and always places black soldiers in the most dangerous positions during patrols.

Judy Duncan An army nurse Richie meets during the trip to Vietnam. Though Richie sees Judy only once more before learning of her death, she serves as the closest thing to a love interest in the novel, and she is a source of confusion and tame fantasy for Richie.

Earlene Peewee's girlfriend. Not long after Peewee arrives in Vietnam, Earlene writes him a letter, informing him that she married another man in his absence. She symbolizes how war disrupts domestic affairs.

Jamal A medic in Richie's company.

Jenkins A member of Richie's squad who arrives in Vietnam at the same time as Richie.

Johnson An extraordinarily strong black soldier on Richie's squad who proves himself to be a born leader.

Johnny Robinson A boy from Richie's neighborhood in Harlem who is killed in Vietnam.

Turner A soldier briefly on Richie's squad.

Walowick A slightly racist soldier on Richie's squad who appears to overcome his prejudices as the bond among the squad members deepens.

ANALYSIS OF MAJOR CHARACTERS

RICHIE PERRY

When Richie Perry first arrives in Vietnam, seventeen years old and fresh out of high school, he is naïve, lost, and confused. He has no grasp on the brutal reality of war, no sense of himself, and no idea of how he wants to build his life. Though he is unusually bright, sensitive, and talented, all of his big dreams—attending college, becoming a writer, giving his brother, Kenny, the opportunities Richie lacked—seem doomed by his poverty. Richie's father abandoned the family years before, leaving the two boys with a depressed and alcoholic mother who spends most of her measly salary on her drinking habit. Richie sees joining the army as his only chance at escape, a way to avoid unsettling questions about himself and his future.

At first, Richie's experience in Vietnam makes him only more doubtful and confused. The carnage, senseless murders, and completely antiheroic nature of the battlefield leave him reeling, adding to his doubts about right and wrong and the morality of the war. Richie struggles with these difficult issues but never finds satisfactory answers. He begins to mature without realizing it and starts to become "the man [he will] be" by asking these complicated questions. Richie's sensitivity and inherent curiosity compel him to reflect on these issues of right and wrong, and also make him the squad's unofficial therapist. He is the friend to whom every soldier in the squad turns when in need of advice or a sympathetic ear. Richie's urgent reactions to his battlefield experiences give him the perspective and insight to become a writer, as they instill in him a compelling need to represent the truth in words, regardless of whether the truth is disturbing or uncomfortable. Returning home after several months of combat, Richie is no closer to solving the problems that plagued him when he left. He is still too poor to attend college and has no means to improve his brother's life, but he has grown from his experiences and started on the path to manhood and emotional maturity.

PEEWEE

Hailing from the brutal streets of the Chicago ghettos, Peewee has learned to respond to fear with a brash humor that either disarms or infuriates anyone who meets him. When Richie first meets Peewee during the trip to Vietnam, Peewee seems arrogant, flippant, and even slightly insane. As the two boys share the experiences of war, however, Richie realizes that Peewee is actually deeply caring, kind, loyal, and tender. While never wholly abandoning his bluster and jokes, Peewee reveals his true self more often as the months drag on, most strikingly after he watches a mother sacrifice her own child in the war effort.

Of all the members of the squad, Peewee best illustrates the odd mixture of boy and man that makes up a soldier. He arrives in Vietnam claiming to have only three goals in life: to drink wine from a corked bottle, to smoke a cigar, and to make love to a foreign woman. Yet later, Peewee also hopes to become the stepfather to his girlfriend's daughter. He is still unable to grow a mustache, and he naïvely puts lotion on his lip to speed its growth. However boyish he is, he also must fight for his country, and he bravely and calmly saves another soldier, Monaco, from death. Like Richie, Peewee leaves Vietnam no closer to figuring out his future, but closer to becoming a man.

LOBEL

As a Jew and a suspected homosexual, Lobel suffers from nearly as much prejudice as his black squad mates. He is thus instantly drawn to Richie and Peewee, and is sympathetic to any racist remarks they receive. The nephew of a Hollywood director, Lobel is obsessed with movies. He incessantly views the war as if it were a movie and at the battlefield as if it were a movie set. He wonders about lighting improvements, set changes, and camera angles. During missions, he imagines himself as an actor playing a role, casting himself as the star of the film so that he is the soldier who does not die. Lobel's fixation on the movies can be seen as an escape from the harsh reality of war. Lobel finds it too difficult to face this reality unprotected, so he desperately clings to the belief that the movies are "the only real thing in life." This belief allows him to dismiss or deny the horror of his experience. Like Peewee's humor, Lobel's obsession with movies is a way to avoid thinking about the tough questions that plague him—complex questions of right and wrong, good and bad, and life and death. By pretending that the world of movies—not the nightmarish world of Vietnam—is real, Lobel tries to convince himself that such difficult questions are not even important. Despite his escapism, Lobel matures during his time in Vietnam. He begins to worry over his skill as a soldier, to take responsibility for the lives of those around him, and, most impressively, to take a deep interest in issues of fairness. When a racist sergeant nearly tears the squad apart, Lobel takes a brave and loyal stand by declaring his allegiance to his black squad mates.

THEMES, MOTIFS & SYMBOLS

THEMES

Themes are the fundamental and often universal ideas explored in a literary work.

THE LOSS OF INNOCENCE

The title of the novel *Fallen Angels* immediately emphasizes the theme of youth and innocence. As Lieutenant Carroll explains in Chapter 4, all soldiers are "angel warriors," because the soldiers are still young boys and still as innocent as angels. In calling the novel *Fallen Angels*, Myers implies that the soldiers' youth and innocence are more important than any of their other aspects, such as their religion, ethnicity, class, or race. The novel is first and foremost a tale of the lost innocence of a squad of soldiers in the Vietnam War. Richie is only seventeen when he enters Vietnam, and Peewee and the other members of the squad are also teenagers—Peewee is unable even to grow a mustache. His three life goals, immaturely, are to drink wine from a corked bottle, to smoke a cigar, and to make love to a foreign woman. Richie and Lobel are both virgins, and they fantasize endlessly about their first sexual experiences.

Though the soldiers enter the war as naïve youths, the war quickly changes them and forces them to develop into young men. Surrounded by death, they are forced to contemplate the fragility of their own lives and stripped of the carelessness and brazenness of youth. The unspeakable horrors around the boys force them to contemplate a world that does not conform to their childish and simplistic notions. Where they want to see only a separation between right and wrong, they instead find moral ambiguity. Where they want to see order and meaning, they find only chaos and senselessness. Where they want to find heroism, they find only the selfish instinct of self-preservation. These realizations destroy the boys' innocence, prematurely thrusting them into manhood.

THE UNROMANTIC REALITY OF WAR

Like all the other soldiers in *Fallen Angels,* Richie joins the army with illusions about what war is like. Like many American civilians, he has learned about war from movies and stories that portray battle as heroic and glorious, the army as efficient and organized, and warfare as a rational effort that depends on skill. What the soldiers actually find in Vietnam bears almost no resemblance to such a mythologized and romanticized version of war. The army is highly inefficient and fallible. Most of the officers are far from heroic, looking out only for their own lives and careers rather than the lives of their soldiers. In the heat of battle, the soldiers think only about self-preservation and ways they can personally survive the onslaught of chaos and violence. Paralyzed by fear, they act blindly and thoughtlessly, often inadvertently killing their allies in the process. The battles and military strategies of the war are disorganized and chaotic, and officers often accidentally reveal their position to the enemy.

Richie, at the beginning of his tour of duty, clings to the myth that the good, smart, and cautious soldiers always survive while enemies, unskilled soldiers, and morally bad people die. The truth is very different, and Richie soon realizes that death is unfair and random, often a matter of pure chance. Richie also has his own personal myths and illusions in addition to the broader societal myths of war. He has, for instance, certain idealized reasons for joining the army: to escape an uncertain and bleak future, to find himself, and to defend freedom and democratic ideals from the threat of Communism. Richie quickly realizes, however, that these preconceived notions about the morality of war are meaningless on the battlefield. When actually in Vietnam, he fights merely to stay alive.

Troubled by this stark gulf between myth and reality, Richie longs to communicate the truth to his family members back home. He wants them to know what war is really like and wants to help them understand what he has experienced. The contrast between the myth and reality of the war makes it almost impossible for him to write to them frankly. He is afraid that they will fail to empathize or understand, since they will cling to the comforting myths they have always embraced. Even worse, Richie fears his family might think poorly of him for failing to live up the unrealistic ideal of the war hero. Though he finally does manage to compose an honest account of battle, he does so only after months of agony.

The Moral Ambiguity of War

Poised to sacrifice their lives for their country, Richie and his fellow soldiers desperately need to believe in a clear-cut distinction between good and bad. They are anxious to confirm that they are in fact on the good side of the conflict, and are not prepared to question whether their cause is the right one. Faced with the horrors he sees around him, Richie cannot help but ask these difficult questions, examining the morality of war and the frequently ambiguous nature of right and wrong. Richie first becomes aware of this moral ambiguity when his squad is sent on a pacification mission to a Vietnamese village. The stated goal of this mission is to convince the villagers that the Americans, and not the Communists, are the good side. This idea disturbs Richie, who reflects, "That was where we were supposed to start from. We, the Americans, were the good guys." Richie feels that the Americans should not have to convince the Vietnamese that they represent the good side. Nonetheless, he recognizes why such a mission is necessary. The American army is responsible—though often inadvertently—for killing many villagers and destroying many villages with their advanced weapons. Regardless of whether the Americans' goal in the war is morally superior to that of their enemies, their localized actions have terrible, immoral consequences.

Richie grows increasingly doubtful about whether American assistance helps the Vietnamese villages, as he sees that the Communist Vietcong retaliate against any villages that receive American aid. Any good that the Americans might do, it seems, leads only to greater evils. As much as they try, the American soldiers cannot protect the South Vietnamese people, and the soldiers' presence only puts the village in greater danger. Richie is no longer able to believe that he is fighting for any clear moral reasons, and he struggles to find meaning for his stay in Vietnam. He finally decides that his only purpose in Vietnam is to stay alive and to help his friends do the same.

MOTIFS

Motifs are recurring structures, contrasts, or literary devices that can help to develop and inform the text's major themes.

RACE

The 1960s were a time of great racial tension in the United States. The African-American civil-rights movement was gaining momentum, and anxieties were growing on all sides. This tension immediately finds its way into the bunker of Richie's squad. The American soldiers frequently trade racial slurs, both about the black soldiers in their midst and about the Vietnamese, who are of a different race than most of the American soldiers. Both manifestations of racism lead to physical violence, with some of the soldiers fighting one another instead of the Vietcong. Yet, as the squad members bond, the prejudices begin to evaporate. Living and fighting very closely, they begin to depend on one another and become able to look past superficial differences. The soldiers come to appreciate one another for their fundamental qualities, and they learn to value each other's humanity and fear for each other's lives. By the time the squad is faced with Sergeant Dongan—a racist who endangers black soldiers because he considers their lives less important—it has come so far that most of the white members are outraged by Dongan's unfair treatment and even offer to risk their own positions by taking a stand against him.

HEROISM

Though the soldiers often talk about heroism, it is almost always part of an effort to denigrate or deflate the concept. Peewee calls heroism stupid and Richie calls it empty. They express the sentiment that a soldier should not try to be heroic and never needlessly risk his life. Nonetheless, the soldiers clearly respect heroism when they see it. When Lieutenant Carroll risks his own life to save a few of his men, the soldiers beneath him revere him more than ever. They admire his heroism but avoid referring to it in noble-sounding terms, saying, "When the chips were down, he put his ass on the line for the guys."

At the same time that they belittle overblown concepts of heroism, the members of the squad also display heroism. Richie repeatedly stresses that he is not a hero. Yet, when given the opportunity to save himself by bowing out of combat duty, he refuses the offer, knowing that his absence would leave his squad short a man, putting them in more danger. Peewee warns Richie not to be "no fucking hero," but when Richie asks Peewee what he would do in the same situation, Peewee admits that he would do the same. Though the squad members have lost any illusion that they are fighting for patriotism or freedom or any other high ideals, they still fight for one another. In putting each other's interests ahead of or on equal ground with their own, they are heroic, despite their protests.

FRIENDSHIP

As the members of Richie's squad become disillusioned with noble and abstract ideals such as patriotism, heroism, and freedom, they find a simpler and more powerful virtue in friendship. Rather than fight for ideas they hardly understand, they simply fight for one another. As Richie reflects, they learn "something . . . about trying to keep each other alive," which supersedes any other reason for fighting. Friendship between the men impels them to incredible acts of bravery. When the squad members are warned that they will be sent on more frequent and more dangerous missions unless they agree to split up, they ignore the warning and stay together. The bond among the squad members grows so strong that they are willing to face greater risks as a team rather than face smaller risks fighting separately. Richie reflects on this bond, because it is this squad of friends that they are really protecting. Without these friends by their side, the squad members have no reason to fight. For them, the war has come to revolve around the squad members.

The growing friendship among the members of the squad also helps them overcome their personal prejudices. When faced with the racist Sergeant Dongan, the squad bands together on the side of the black soldiers. When Dongan questions Johnson about Lobel's homosexuality, Johnson does not respond, later explaining to Richie that he could not care less whether Lobel is a homosexual because any man fighting by his side is equally an ally, regardless of the nature of his personal life. By living and fighting so closely together, the men are able to overcome their petty biases and appreciate and support one another.

MOTIFS

SYMBOLS

Symbols are objects, characters, figures, or colors used to represent abstract ideas or concepts.

RICHIE'S LETTERS HOME

The letters Richie writes home symbolize his changing attitude toward the myths of war. At first, he fully believes in these myths and has little trouble writing home, sending carefree and optimistic messages about the coming truce and the souvenirs he plans to bring home with him. Once in Vietnam, as the illusions begin to fade, Richie suddenly finds writing to be a painful exercise. Confused by the sharp difference between the myth and reality of war, he finds himself at a loss for words. His letters strike him as dishonest, since they avoid the difficult issues and take on false and often humorous tones. Richie struggles to reconcile his earlier beliefs with his current experiences and finds himself unable to communicate his thoughts and feelings. As his confusion disperses and he forces himself to see war in all its stark, brutal reality, he is finally able to write a truthful and frank letter. Richie's letters once again become an honest representation of his thoughts and feelings, indicating that he has sorted out the chaos, gained a clear perspective, and is ready to seek out truths about war and himself.

THE LOST DOG TAGS

In the midst of one terrible battle, when time is short and the men must evacuate immediately, they are forced to burn the bodies of the victims. In the tumult to escape, they lose the dog tags—military identification tags—of these dead soldiers and are left with no physical evidence of these men's lives and deaths. The loss of the dog tags is highly symbolic, emphasizing the complete anonymity and obscurity of a soldier's death. It illustrates the tragedy of any lost soldier; though the myths may claim that each soldier dies with dignity and meaning, in reality some soldiers die in obscurity, with no reason for their deaths aside from pure chance. Richie comes to understand that each soldier's death swallows up his previous victories and sacrifices, which are anonymous and quickly forgotten.

WAR MOVIES

War movies are full of worn-out notions about war that are common in American popular culture. As such, they are both a primary source and a symbol of the mythology of warfare that pervades civilian life, which includes clichés such as the tragic death of the baby-faced virgin soldier or the consistently positive portrait of the black soldier. These films reveal the American tendency to beautify and romanticize real wartime tragedies, attaching false meaning to deaths that are often senseless, random, and brutal. Such movies also tend to force the two sides of the conflict into clear divisions—black and white, good and evil, right and wrong—even though the nature of war is often highly ambiguous, with the seemingly just or moral cause not always emerging as the victorious one. Lobel's obsession with movies suggests that he seeks to glorify war. He does not really understand war's true nature, and he perhaps does not even wish to understand it. Rather, he prefers to believe in a romanticized notion of war in which soldiers are heroic and enjoy the deep bonds of camaraderie with their fellow men in life and are afforded dignity in death.

SYMBOLS

SUMMARY & ANALYSIS

CHAPTERS 1–3

SUMMARY: CHAPTER 1

It is 1967 and seventeen-year-old Richie Perry, a black high school graduate from Harlem, joins the army. He has few other choices: though he is very intelligent, his single mother, abandoned by her husband years ago, cannot afford to send him to college. Rather than remain in the slums of Harlem, Richie enlists in the army amid rumors of impending peace—he thinks that the Vietnam War will end before he even has to fire a gun. While in basic training, he injures his knee playing basketball, earning him a medical profile that should keep him out of combat. However, due to a paperwork mishap, Richie's file is not properly processed, and he is sent to Vietnam anyway. His captain assures him that the file will soon be processed and that he will be sent home without ever seeing actual combat.

On the trip over, Richie befriends Judy Duncan, an army nurse, and Harold Gates, a cocky young black soldier from Chicago whom his friends call Peewee. The plane stops overnight in Osaka, Japan, and due to another bureaucratic mishap, the soldiers are forced to pay for their own dinners and sleep on benches in the airport. Richie feels unease at these signs of what he sees as the army's general incompetence. He buys a souvenir for his younger brother, Kenny. When he finally arrives in Vietnam, Richie is separated from Judy Duncan, but is assigned to the same barracks as Peewee. Though the sound of artillery in the distance makes him anxious, Richie is somewhat comforted by the fact that the camp in Vietnam looks exactly like his basic-training facility back in Massachusetts.

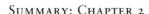

Summary: Chapter 2

All the other guys in the neighborhood thought I was
going to college. I wasn't, and the army was the place
I was going to get away from all the questions.

(See QUOTATIONS, p. 45)

Lying in bed, Richie reflects that he joined the army in part to earn money to send home to Kenny, and in part to avoid tough questions about his impossible dreams for the future. Over breakfast the next morning, Peewee tells Richie that he likes the army because for the first time in his life he has exactly what everyone else has—the same clothing, shoes, food, and so on. A large African-American soldier named Rings approaches Richie and Peewee and asks them to cut their skin so that they can all become blood brothers. He explains that they need to stick together as fellow blacks. When Richie and Peewee refuse to do as Rings asks, he calls them Uncle Toms.

Later in the day, Peewee and Richie speak with an experienced soldier who further confirms the rumor of a coming truce. Richie writes a letter to Kenny, telling him that the war is going to end very soon. After killing time at the base for ten days, Richie, Peewee, and a terrified young man named Jenkins are finally assigned to a camp near Chu Lai. On the truck headed for their new squad, Peewee says he is not afraid, but Richie can tell that Peewee is just as frightened as he is. Jenkins begins crying, which calms Richie, who feels braver by comparison.

Summary: Chapter 3

Once they arrive at the base near Chu Lai, the boys meet Johnson, an extraordinarily strong black soldier from Savannah, Georgia. Johnson takes offense when Peewee mocks Georgia, and there is tension in their relationship from the start. Jenkins reveals that he is in the army only because his father, a colonel, wants him to begin a military career. He confesses to Richie that he is convinced he is going to die, but Richie assures him that most soldiers never fire their guns.

The four soldiers finally arrive at their new base. The commanding officer tells Richie that his medical file has not yet arrived. Richie tries to write a letter home but cannot find the right words. That night, Richie, Peewee, and Jenkins go on night patrol with their squad. Simpson, the squad sergeant, warns the new soldiers not to get him killed because of their inexperience, as he is just four months away from completing his tour of duty. The patrol is more terrifying than Richie had ever expected, but goes smoothly until the very end. Just as they are reentering their camp, Jenkins steps on a land mine, and is killed instantly.

ANALYSIS: CHAPTERS 1–3

The opening chapters of Fallen Angels immediately introduce the stark difference between the romantic, idealized concept of war and the harsh reality of it. Richie, Peewee, and the other soldiers in their squad enlist in the army for reasons that are vague at best, and they have an even less clear idea of what war is really like. Richie believes that the army and war follow a rational plan, which causes him to expect that his medical profile will be processed promptly and correctly and that he will not have to go into combat. He also believes that peace is not far off and that most soldiers do not actually fire their guns anyway. On the whole, in these first chapters, it is clear that Richie does not have a realistic view of the inefficiency, chaos, and hopeless unpredictability of war.

Richie becomes suspicious about the lack of the army's control during the layover in Osaka. He is frightened by the consequences of the army's mistakes and begins to suspect that the myths about the heroism and morality of war are as misleading as the myths about military competence and efficiency. When Richie arrives in Chu Lai, he begins to see that the war effort is consistently characterized by petty careerism and fear, rather than by noble or heroic acts. Sergeant Simpson's only goal is to get out of Vietnam alive, regardless of his men's safety. Likewise, Captain Stewart, as we see in the next chapter, deliberately and unnecessarily risks the lives of the soldiers in Richie's company in an attempt to get promoted. Neither of these officers is concerned with the ideals the United States uses to justify its involvement in Vietnam. Rather, the officers care only about their own safety and ambitions. Jenkins's death reinforces the idea that war is cruel, senseless, and unromantic.

Another major idea in these opening chapters is that of lost innocence. Richie, Peewee, and the others are still teenage boys, even though in Vietnam they must act like adults. They are still largely sheltered and innocent. We learn later that Peewee's three major goals in life are to drink wine from a corked bottle, to make love to a foreign woman, and to smoke a cigar. Peewee's aims are stereotypically male goals, showing that he still clings to vague ideas of what it means to be a man and that he has not yet matured into his own person with unique ambitions. Richie is similarly naïve, spending his first days in Vietnam thinking of buying Kenny a souvenir, as if his tour of duty were a vacation. Despite the false comfort provided by rumors of peace talks, Richie and Peewee are frightened and confused, and they react to this fear and uncertainty in childish ways. Peewee copes with his emotions with a mixture of bravado and humor. Richie clings to false illusions, irrationally hoping that his file will be processed and he will be sent home before he has to enter combat. By emphasizing the youth and innocence of these characters, Myers illustrates the tragedy of war—its transformation of teenage boys into killers for a cause that they often do not even understand.

These opening chapters also illustrate the sharp racial and economic divisions in American society during the Vietnam era. The burden of the war fell largely on youth from working-class and minority populations. College students—predominantly from white, middle-class backgrounds—were exempt from the draft. Richie chooses to enlist in the army only because he is too poor to attend college, and Peewee is a high school dropout. The rest of the squad also hails from less affluent segments of the American population, either from minority groups or from rural states. Peewee declares that he likes being in the army because the army is the only place where everyone has what he has. Though Peewee might consider the army a great equalizer, he joins the army and risks his life only because he has so little to begin with, whereas more fortunate boys his age can safely prepare for their futures at college. Myers subtly but effectively emphasizes this often overlooked irony: the men with the least access to America's freedoms and privileges are the ones sent to war to defend American ideals against Communism. These soldiers are fighting to preserve the American dream—an idea strongly rooted in the acquisition of material wealth—even though this dream is largely unavailable to them.

CHAPTERS 4–6

SUMMARY: CHAPTER 4

"My father used to call all soldiers angel warriors," he said. "Because usually they get boys to fight wars. Most of you aren't old enough to vote yet."

(See QUOTATIONS, p. 46)

Lieutenant Carroll, the kind and competent leader of the platoon, leads a moving prayer for Jenkins, calling him an "angel warrior." Carroll explains that his own father, also a military man, used to call all soldiers "angel warriors" because so many soldiers are young and as innocent as angels. Richie tries to write a letter home about Jenkins's death, but he finds the subject too difficult to broach, and decides to write about Peewee instead.

The next few days are slow, giving the members of the squad time for conversations about their lives and their hopes for the future. An Italian soldier named Monaco tells the others about his days as a star high school athlete, an African-American soldier named Brew discusses his intention to become a priest, and a Jewish boy from California named Lobel talks about his love of movies. Soon, the squad is sent on a public-relations mission, bringing food and medical supplies to a Vietnamese village. Lobel and Richie befriend a young Vietnamese girl named An Linh. Peewee buys a bottle of wine, telling the others that one of his three life goals is to drink wine from a bottle with a cork; the other two are to smoke a cigar and to make love to a foreign woman. Back at the base, Sergeant Simpson complains to Peewee and Richie that the leader of their company, Captain Stewart, wants to embroil them in more dangerous missions for a selfish reason—he can be promoted to major only if he increases the enemy body count.

SUMMARY: CHAPTER 5

Peewee receives a letter from his girlfriend, Earlene, informing him that she has married another man in his absence. After a few quiet days spent watching and rewatching a Julie Andrews movie and listening to the rumors of peace talks on the radio, the squad is sent on a mission that proves uneventful. Afterward, Lieutenant Carroll approaches Richie about his still unprocessed profile. He gives Richie a chance to remove himself from combat permanently by asking him to assess how bad his injury is. Out of a growing sense of loyalty to the members of his squad, Richie refuses to take advantage of this easy way out of danger.

SUMMARY: CHAPTER 6

Richie and Lobel are put on guard duty. Lobel, whose uncle is a film director, tries to convince Richie that movies are the only real thing in life. He confesses that whenever he goes on patrol, he imagines that he is playing the part of a soldier in a movie. He dissects the various war movie clichés for Richie. Lobel laments, for instance, that he is still a virgin, since the baby-faced virgin always dies in war movies. He suggests that Richie avoid playing the part of the good black guy who everyone thinks is a coward until the end, when he dies while saving everyone else. Richie confesses to Lobel that he wishes he had a girlfriend so he could have another person with whom to exchange letters. Lobel offers to give him the address of a movie starlet, but Richie is not interested in a pretend girlfriend.

A news crew comes to interview Richie's squad. They ask each soldier to explain why he is fighting in Vietnam. Each soldier gives a different stock response, citing lofty and slightly abstract goals such as the desire to stem the spread of Communism. When Richie's turn comes, he tells the reporters that he is fighting in Vietnam to prevent fighting in the streets of America. The news crew later accompanies Richie's squad on patrol. Monaco, who always acts as point man for the squad, leads the others and kills an enemy soldier, while Richie tries to fire a gun that he forgot to load. Back at camp Richie finds the news crew photographing the dead soldier and is astonished that the enemy is no bigger than his brother, Kenny.

ANALYSIS: CHAPTERS 4–6

Lobel's commentary on war movies highlights the contrast between the myth and reality of warfare. War movies exhibit the clichés common in American popular culture—the tragic death of the baby-faced virgin soldier and the inevitably positive portrait of the black soldier. Such movies tend to infuse senseless deaths with false meaning, giving us beautiful, romantic representations of our favorite myths about good, evil, and heroism. These romanticized myths can help society deal with wartime loss by providing a justification for soldiers' sacrifices, but these same myths also gloss over the ugliness and horror that are everywhere in war. In this sense, these myths do not give justice to the sacrifices expected of the soldiers fighting in reality.

These war myths also make it difficult for the soldier to share his burden of fear and suffering with his family, which leaves him feeling isolated and alienated from civilian life. Richie finds himself unable to write a satisfactory letter to his mother and Kenny because he does not know how to communicate his thoughts and feelings. His family's beliefs about war are in line with the popular, idealized myths. Richie is afraid that they will not understand what he is feeling and that they will think less of him for abandoning the abstract ideals that make sense to them. In his loneliness and intense need to communicate, Richie seizes on the idea of having a girlfriend, thinking that a girlfriend would be able to understand what he has been through and would connect him to the rest of humanity by allowing him to share his fears. Richie also needs to feel that there are people who care about him and understand him, people who will help him return to a normal life after he leaves Vietnam.

Richie, however, no longer believes in the war myths propagated by movies and books. When he turns down the opportunity to be removed from combat, he is not acting out of any false illusions of wartime heroism and abstract ideals, but out of a genuine sense of fairness and friendship. Richie knows that dying while trying to be a hero would be senseless, not brave or noble. Yet he has become close friends with the men on his squad and feels obligated to them. If he were to back out of combat duty, his squad would be short another man and be in more danger during combat and patrol missions. Richie's combat experiences have replaced his original reasons for fighting the war, such as heroism and patriotism, with the less lofty—but perhaps more substantive—ideals of loyalty and friendship.

Richie's first exposure to the death of an enemy soldier further shatters his romanticized myths of war. Richie is shocked to see that the soldier is no bigger than Kenny—the enemies are boys, just like the American soldiers. Richie realizes that each side dehumanizes the enemy to justify or rationalize the mass killings involved in war. When he sees the dead Vietcong soldier in front of him, he humanizes the enemy in his mind and wonders what his life was like. When the news crew interviews Richie's squad, the soldiers give varying reasons for being in Vietnam, but all of them are borrowed from the popular war rhetoric that permeates the American media. After seeing the enemy as human beings, Richie begins to search for his own reasons for being in Vietnam. He wants to find his own meaning in his war experiences. Walowick reminds Richie that the only real goal in the heat of combat is to survive. Communism, patriotism, and democratic ideals are meaningless when a soldier is faced with an enemy rifle.

CHAPTERS 7–9

SUMMARY: CHAPTER 7

Jamal, a medic, informs Richie that Captain Stewart has reported three kills for the patrol despite the fact that really only one enemy was killed. Richie wonders about the dead soldier's family, his life, and his hopes for the future. Walowick, another member of the squad, urges him to stop worrying about the dead soldier; the only thing that matters is that Richie himself is still alive. Richie comes down with a terrible intestinal disease and spends several days recovering. Johnson and Walowick get into a racially charged fight when Walowick calls Johnson a "cootie." Peewee asks Richie to write a letter to Earlene on his behalf, since it is too painful for him to write it himself. Because Richie misses a patrol with his own squad while he is sick, he is sent on patrol with another company.

SUMMARY: CHAPTER 8

During a patrol with a different company, Richie's squad accidentally opens fire on one of its own platoons, killing more than a dozen American soldiers. Richie is distraught that so many people are dead because of this sheer carelessness. Later, Richie approaches Lieutenant Carroll to ask where he can buy a knife to send as a birthday present to Kenny. Lieutenant Carroll gives Richie a beautiful silk jacket to send to Kenny instead. Haunted by the scenes of chaos and confusion that he has witnessed, Richie asks Brew to show him where the Lord's Prayer can be found in the Bible. Brew lends Richie his Bible.

SUMMARY: CHAPTER 9

*I didn't like having to convince anybody that I was
the good guy. That was where we were supposed to
start from.*   (See QUOTATIONS, p. 47)

The bossy Corporal Brunner tells the squad that it is going on a pacification mission to another village. The squad members must convince the villagers that they, and not the Communists, are their allies
in the conflict. Richie is disturbed that there is any doubt about
which side is good, but he needs to believe that his side is unques-
tionably in the right. He is further bothered by the fact that the villagers are afraid of him and his friends. Richie does not want to
think of himself as a frightening killer and cringes when Lobel com-
pares the squad to outlaws from cowboy movies. During an other-
wise uneventful mission, Peewee buys several homemade remedies
from a villager, including a potion that is supposed to encourage
hair growth. Back at the base, the squad members are happy to learn
that they are going on another pacification mission the following
day. Hours later they find out that this mission has been assigned to
another group: Captain Stewart does not want his soldiers going on
pacification missions because these relatively safe missions do not
add to the enemy body count.

Peewee receives an apologetic letter from Earlene, telling him
that she plans to name her next child after him. Lobel receives an
angry letter from his father that is filled with antiwar sentiment.
Lobel laments the irony of his situation: he joined the army to please
his father by proving that he is not a homosexual, and now his father
hates him for becoming a soldier in what he regards as an unjust war.
Richie receives a letter from Kenny, who wants to join a basketball
league but does not have enough money to enroll. Richie sends the
money immediately. He feels good that Kenny still needs him.

Two female American Red Cross workers come to the camp, and
one of them asks Richie what he is going to do when he gets home.
The question mortifies him and sends him into a painful recollection
of an episode in high school when a guidance counselor laughed at
him for saying he wanted to be a philosopher. Ever since then, he
reflects, the question of his future has made him feel uncomfortable.

ANALYSIS: CHAPTERS 7–9
Richie's discomfort about his unknown future grows worse as his
disillusionment with Vietnam increases. He first enters the army to

avoid the tough questions about who he is and what he will do with his future. Now, faced with the reality of war, he wants to look forward to civilian life, but finds himself unable to see his future. Though most of Richie's discomfort about the future stems from his lack of options, it also stems partly from confusion about his identity and his disappointment with the army. Richie has hoped that the army would help him find in himself the man he feels destined to become. As it turns out, he faces nothing but brutality, fear, and chaos, and realizes that he will not find himself in the army. He looks enviously to men like Johnson and Monaco, who seem to have found their true selves in the army—Monaco is the brave point man and Johnson is the strong machine gunner and born leader. Richie no longer harbors any illusions of following in their footsteps and figuring out his true self. Vietnam, he realizes, has none of the answers, and only offers more questions.

Unlike soldiers in almost any other war, the soldiers who fought in Vietnam did not have the benefit of a grateful nation behind them. For their ultimate sacrifice, the soldiers earned mainly disdain and contempt from a public who viewed the war largely as unethical. Lobel's father's antiwar sentiments add another touch of cruelty to the soldiers' situation in Vietnam. Though Brunner angrily rants later on about the "faggots and Commies" back home who oppose the war effort, none of the boys in the squad knows how virulent and widespread the antiwar sentiment truly is. The squad members still cling to the belief that when they return home the nation will hail them as heroes. The brief mentions of war protest scattered throughout the novel deepen our sympathy for the characters by emphasizing another tragic aspect of their position in the war.

Richie is keenly aware of the hypocrisy of the pacification missions—even though he is armed with grenades and automatic weapons, he is supposed to convince Vietnamese villagers that the Americans represent the good side by handing out food and medical supplies. From the villagers' point of view, the Americans and their allies do not seem any different from the Vietcong guerrillas who punish and torture them for accepting the food and medicine. Yet Richie is upset when Lobel points out that, from the point of view of many Vietnamese, the Americans are just like the killers who ride into town in cowboy movies. Despite his crumbling illusions, Richie still does not want to believe that the war is morally ambiguous. He still wants to believe that the war is right and that he and his fellow soldiers are the good guys.

CHAPTERS 10–12

SUMMARY: CHAPTER 10

In retaliation for receiving aid from American soldiers, the Communist Vietcong attack the nearby village that Richie's squad has
recently pacified. Richie's company creeps up on the village to set an
ambush for the Vietcong. Feeling exposed and vulnerable, Richie
wonders how Kenny would feel if Richie died, and ponders his own
motivations for joining the army, trying to decide whether they were
selfless or selfish. He tries to take his mind off these weighty and
upsetting thoughts by fantasizing about beautiful women. But he
begins to worry about the fact that he is still a virgin, feeling inade-
quate because of the hypersexualized stereotypes of black men.
During the ambush, Richie fires blindly into the darkness. Lieutenant Carroll is hit by enemy fire and dies shortly after they reach the
hospital at Chu Lai.

SUMMARY: CHAPTER 11

> We spent another day lying around. It seemed to be
> what the war was about. Hours of boredom, seconds
> of terror.   (See QUOTATIONS, p. 48)

The squad members are in shock after Carroll's death, since they
have lost someone whom they all loved and respected. At Simpson's
request, Richie writes a letter to Carroll's pregnant wife informing
her of her husband's death. Richie wonders how his mother and
Kenny would react if they received a letter about his death. Stewart
praises Richie for the letter he writes to Carroll's wife and offers him
an office job, but Richie refuses.

As usual, there are hours of inactivity after the brief but traumatic periods of combat. During a slow period, Lobel approaches
Richie and admits that he holds himself responsible for Carroll's
death. He was too afraid to fire his weapon during the ambush, and
he believes, irrationally, that his ineptitude is what caused Carroll to
die. Richie consoles Lobel by admitting that, even though he fired,
he fired blindly.

Every squad member is promoted one rank for his valiant perfor-
mance in a dangerous situation. Richie spends tortured hours trying
to find a meaningful reason for Carroll's death. He wonders why he
and his fellow soldiers are so far from home. He starts but does not

finish a letter to Kenny trying to give a reason for his own death in case he is killed. The platoon is assigned a new leader, Lieutenant Gearhart, who has been in Vietnam for only two months. Richie's mother writes to Peewee and asks him to tell Richie that she loves him very much. Richie is sad that she is unable to express her feelings directly to him, and writes a letter telling his mother that he loves her too. Richie realizes that though they have never gotten along well, he desperately needs his mother now. When the news feature about Richie's squad airs, no one mentions the fact that Lieutenant Carroll is shown walking among them, still alive.

SUMMARY: CHAPTER 12

Brunner expresses his anger at the "faggots and Commies" back in the United States who burn their draft cards. He blames them for the constant shortage of men in the squads. Johnson later asks Richie for his opinion about the war protesters. They both admit that neither has thought much about his decision to enlist. Richie confesses that he is no longer sure who the good guys and bad guys are, since all the talk about freedom and Communism ceases to mean anything in the heat of combat. Johnson tells him that there is no meaning to Vietnam and suggests that Richie stop thinking about these larger issues. As he falls asleep later that night, Richie wonders whether people can still be good.

ANALYSIS: CHAPTERS 10–12

In the absence of any rational explanation, Richie struggles to understand the war. The newspaper and television rhetoric that justifies the war means nothing to a soldier who comes face to face with an armed enemy. The war appears to be futile: Richie's company continually tries to pacify villages with gifts of food and medicine, but the Vietcong torture and kill villagers who accept these gifts, and the American army is unable to protect them. The war has no simple divisions between heroes and villains, good and evil, or right and wrong. Instead, the war is a messy, brutal tangle of deadly mistakes and confrontations in which blind chance often determines who lives and who dies. The other soldiers in the squad accept the irrationality and meaninglessness of combat and force themselves not to ponder questions that have no answers. Johnson, in fact, regards Richie's philosophical struggle as a dangerous distraction. Johnson does not care why he is in Vietnam; his only goal is survival, and he is not fighting for anything other than his own life. Yet Richie cannot stop thinking about the war's meaning and is compelled to find meaning and order amid the chaos.

The letters from the military troop to their loved ones back home reinforce the myths of war and provide meaning to their overseas experience. Richie's letter to Lieutenant Carroll's wife, like his letters to his mother and to Kenny, is a sanitized narrative meant to shield the recipient from pain. Richie politely praises Carroll's service and expresses regret at having to report his death. The letter appeals to popular myths of war, giving Carroll's death meaning by characterizing it as a brave man's sacrifice for his country. In stark contrast to the sanitized version invented by Richie, Carroll's actual death provokes intense anxiety and doubt in the men under his command. For them, there is no easy, comprehensible reason for Carroll's death. Groping blindly, guiltily, and fearfully for answers, Lobel even feels that he might be at fault for Carroll's death, as if his own terror could somehow have killed his leader. Though Richie knows that the myths of warfare fail to represent the realities of the war, he is wise and sensitive enough to recognize that these myths are useful for relating tragic news. He is becoming as savvy as his superiors in the army, learning how to wield untruths successfully while not falling prey to their seductive power.

As warfare changes Richie, he begins to feel strongly that he needs to mend his relationship with his mother. Richie has never felt close to his mother because of her alcoholism, and Kenny is the only one in his family with whom he feels a strong connection. Now, however, as the terrors of war become more salient, Richie realizes that he needs as many human connections as possible, and what he seeks from his mother is the sort of maternal protection that mothers instinctively offer their children. The letter that Richie's mother sends to Peewee causes Richie to change his relationship with her. He finally writes a meaningful letter to his mother, one that expresses his feelings and begins to heal their damaged relationship.

CHAPTERS 13–16

SUMMARY: CHAPTER 13

Christmas is approaching and rumors of peace have reached a fever pitch. The North Vietnamese have supposedly called a truce for their new year, called the Tet, and this truce is expected to lengthen into a permanent cease-fire. Everyone is convinced that the American troops will be returning home in a matter of weeks. Richie writes a letter telling his mother the good news. Meanwhile, the squad hears reports of considerable racial tension at home. Though the squad makes sure to steer clear of the subject, everyone is very aware of the race-related incidents. There have been riots in New York over the killing of a black teenager by a white police officer, and Richie hopes that Kenny is being careful. During his first patrol with the squad, Gearhart accidentally exposes the squad's position to the enemy, and a new member of the squad, Turner, is killed as a result.

SUMMARY: CHAPTER 14

Gearhart writes a letter to Turner's parents blaming himself for their son's death. At Captain Stewart's request, Richie rewrites the letter. Instinctively knowing what Stewart wants him to write, Richie claims in the letter that Turner died while valiantly trying to save his fellow soldiers. In his official report, Stewart once again exaggerates the number of enemies killed during patrol. Monaco's girlfriend proposes to him in a letter, and the squad votes that he should marry her. Monaco invites everyone to the wedding.

Soon after, Richie's company is sent back to the village they recently tried to pacify, since the Vietcong have been harassing the village again. When they arrive, the Vietcong have already struck, leaving behind mutilated bodies and burnt huts in their wake. Richie enters a hut where a Vietcong takes him by surprise. The Vietcong's gun misfires and Richie shoots him point blank. Back at camp, the soldiers find it difficult to calm down after seeing so much carnage and destruction. Richie is especially shaken after watching a man die by his hands. Peewee and Richie sleep in the same bed for mutual comfort that night. Soon thereafter, Richie's company is ordered to a new base near Tam Ky. The day that they are supposed to leave, Peewee wakes up with a swollen face. The others hound him, and he finally admits that he put the Vietnamese hair serum on his lip in the hope of growing a mustache.

SUMMARY: CHAPTER 15

Richie tries to write a letter to Kenny about killing the Vietcong, but he cannot find the right words. He cannot explain the war in terms of good and bad or of stopping the spread of Communism, so he simply gives up.

The new base at Tam Ky is far more primitive than the one at Chu Lai, and night patrols there are also more dangerous. While on patrol, Richie wonders about the man he has killed, focusing on the question of what his victim thought he was fighting for. He wonders whether the Vietcong soldier would have said that he was trying to stop the spread of what the Americans stand for. During the patrol, Richie's squad runs into dozens of enemy soldiers. The squad members silently hide because they are far too outnumbered to try an ambush. Under pressure from Stewart, Simpson extends the tour of duty by thirty days. Tensions build between the Americans and their Vietnamese allies at the camp. During a battle, Brew is mortally wounded and Richie is hit in the leg and wrist.

SUMMARY: CHAPTER 16
The medics load Brew and Richie into an evacuation helicopter. While the medics work on Richie's wounds, he holds Brew's hand as Brew dies. Richie is transferred to a recovery hospital, where life is routine and quiet. In a letter to his mother, he tries to joke about his injury because he does not want to tell her what the experience of being hit was really like or how terrified he was of dying. Richie finds that Judy Duncan is stationed in the hospital's nursing unit, and they share a short chat. The army awards Richie a Purple Heart for his injury. He sends the medal to Kenny, along with a letter outlining all the things he plans to do with him when he gets home. Richie receives orders to return to his unit and briefly considers going AWOL (absent without leave) because he does not think he can tolerate the fear and uncertainty of battle anymore.

SUMMARY & ANALYSIS

ANALYSIS: CHAPTERS 13–16
Since his arrival in Vietnam, Richie's experience with the violence and brutality of the war has become more and more personal and traumatic. At first, he is shaken by Jenkins's sudden, senseless death, even though he never knew Jenkins well. Later, seeing Monaco kill an enemy soldier forces Richie to question the morality of war. Because Richie does not kill this enemy soldier himself, he is able to contemplate these moral questions with some emotional distance. When Carroll dies, Richie is forced to consider the war in light of losing people he cares about and knows well. However, after Richie kills an enemy soldier face to face, he must wrestle with the fact that he himself has taken the life of another person. Though he knows

that he has killed the soldier only to save his own life, he cannot help thinking that a man is dead by his hand. Richie does not think of himself as a hero now that he has killed a Vietcong. He cannot yet tell Kenny about the incident because he is still emotionally and morally conflicted about it. He no longer has distance from the brutality and moral ambiguity of war—he has become a part of it.

As the horror of war increasingly pervades the squad, the love and friendship between the soldiers deepen, and these bonds keep the young men sane and give them reason to fight. The squad becomes like a family, with each soldier trying to save not only his own life but also the lives of all his brothers. Monaco trusts and respects his fellow soldiers so much that he allows them to vote on important decisions in his life; when the squad votes that he should marry his girlfriend, he takes the result as non-negotiable. The love and tenderness between the soldiers become even more apparent when Richie's first killing traumatizes him. Peewee embraces Richie like a mother, father, or brother would, and they fall asleep holding on to each other. The bond growing over the course of these chapters culminates with Brew's death. As Brew struggles to live, he extends his hand toward Richie, who grasps it, trying to communicate through his grip all the sentiments that he feels unable to communicate through words. Richie begins to realize, as he grips Brew's hand, that the only unambiguous virtue in war is loyalty to one's fellow soldiers.

Peewee's faith in the hair lotion he puts on his lip emphasizes the fact that the soldiers, despite their war experience, are still largely innocent boys. The event is somewhat jarring in its placement, since it reminds us of the soldiers' innocence just when they are about to be sent on a dangerous and important mission, taking their own lives and the lives of their friends in their hands. They face their new mission stoically and seem like men, but the episode with Peewee reminds us that they are still boys. Peewee does not even have a mustache yet, and his attempt to grow one with the hair ointment is so silly and immature that it is hard to believe he makes life and death decisions every day. This episode underscores the fact that war expects boys to do a job that few grown men can accomplish.

CHAPTERS 17–19

SUMMARY: CHAPTER 17

Richie returns to his unit and learns that Sergeant Simpson has finally gone home. The new squad sergeant, Dongan, is a racist who consistently puts black soldiers in the most dangerous positions during patrols. Lobel approaches Peewee and Richie to tell them that he is on their side if a serious race problem breaks out within the squad. Richie receives a letter from Peewee's old girlfriend, Earlene, apologizing for marrying another man. Afraid that Peewee will find the letter and be hurt all over again, Richie burns it. Kenny writes and reports that he has taken a part-time job. He also mentions that Johnny Robinson, a neighborhood boy, has been killed in Vietnam. Richie is shocked that someone who looked so young could have been in Vietnam.

The Vietnamese allies find a woman walking with two children along the rice paddies surrounding the base camp. American soldiers bring her to the camp, but there is no interpreter around to question her. Most of the American soldiers are sympathetic to the mother, thinking that she is being unfairly detained at their camp. Peewee hurries to make the woman's children a doll out of grass. Just as he finishes the doll, the woman hands one of her children to a soldier. Seconds later, the child explodes in the soldier's arms, killing him. The child had been equipped with mines by his mother, made into a weapon, and sacrificed. The American soldiers then shoot down the woman and her second child.

SUMMARY: CHAPTER 18

Johnson tells Richie that Dongan approached him to inquire whether Lobel was a homosexual. Johnson reports that he did not give an answer, since he feels that what Lobel does in bed is not his concern. Johnson considers each man fighting by his side an appreciated ally. Richie reflects that Johnson is a born leader who has also learned much by fighting alongside others.

Tensions between the American soldiers and their Vietnamese allies heighten when a Vietnamese colonel insists that the Americans try to capture a crucial hill. Richie's company climbs the hill without encountering enemy soldiers and then returns to regroup with the Vietnamese soldiers. When they climb the hill again, the Vietnamese soldiers take the lead. This time, enemy soldiers attack the squad members. The squad attempts to secure a nearby village in order to evacuate the area, and Dongan is killed during the fight.

SUMMARY: CHAPTER 19

Richie's company has still not been evacuated, but he and his fellow squad members know they need to leave as soon as possible because a North Vietnamese battalion is coming to the village. The company strips the tags and gear off dead American soldiers and burns the bodies. One soldier is still alive, but his wounds are clearly mortal, so one of his friends shoots him out of mercy while everyone scrambles to escape. All of the dead soldiers' identification tags are lost in the confusion. Richie imagines writing a letter to the families of the dead, telling them how their sons' bodies were burned in the forest while their comrades fled in fear and panic. During the race to the choppers, Jamal freezes in sudden panic until Gearhart shouts at him to start moving again. Richie feels as if there is someone else in his body running for his life. He wishes he could watch the rest of the war like a movie.

ANALYSIS: CHAPTERS 17–19

One of the most torturous aspects of war is the common soldier's lack of control over his life. We feel this utter helplessness of the soldier in the face of fate vividly when the army forces Richie to return to his unit after a peaceful period of recuperation. He desperately wants to avoid this fate, feeling that he is psychologically and emotionally unable to face any more combat. Yet he has no choice but to return, since he has effectively relinquished control over his life upon joining the army. The soldiers are similarly helpless in the face of the dangerous careerism of men like Captain Stewart and the racism of Sergeant Dongan. Stewart forces his company to take the most dangerous missions so that he can be promoted to major, and Dongan forces minority soldiers in his squad to take the most dangerous jobs because he considers them expendable. Though the soldiers know that Dongan's treatment of the black soldiers is unfair and that Stewart's treatment of the entire company is selfish, they cannot change these men's decisions. The army is a rigid hierarchy in which inferiors can never question or challenge the orders of superiors.

The camaraderie among the members of the squad begins to overcome their social prejudices. Lobel declares that he will side with the black soldiers against the racist Dongan should the need arise. Monaco displays similar loyalty to the black soldiers. Johnson is indifferent toward Lobel's sexual orientation, declaring that any soldier who fights beside him is an ally, regardless of his personal preferences. This statement of tolerance illustrates the squad members' need to support one another, despite their differences. By living and fighting so closely, the soldiers become able to look past superficial differences and appreciate one another for their fundamental human qualities. Richie says that they are "trying to keep each other alive," suggesting that they fully appreciate each other's humanity above anything else.

Myers also suggests that wartime standards of morality are dramatically different from civilian standards of morality. The incident with the exploding child reminds us that there are aspects of war that are unthinkable during peacetime. In the madness of the war, a mother will sacrifice even her own child for the sake of killing just one enemy soldier. The incident redraws the blurred lines between the side of good and the side of bad, as the American soldiers believe that their side would never encourage a mother to use her child as a weapon. In this sense, the incident helps the soldiers regain the feeling that they are on the side of good. Yet the incident does not satisfy Richie's questions about the moral ambiguity of war. After all, the mother would never have been compelled to perform such a horrible action if the Americans were not fighting in Vietnam. Like all the other portrayals of battle in the novel, the mother's sacrifice of her child neither condemns nor justifies the war in Vietnam, but it raises a new set of difficult and important questions.

The loss of the dead soldiers' dog tags has similarly profound repercussions for Richie's emotional state. The loss of these tags is highly symbolic: with the bodies burned and the dog tags lost, there is literally nothing left of the soldiers who have died. Their identities have been erased as if they never existed at all. Richie instantly recognizes that the event represents the tragedy of any lost soldier. Although the idealized version of war may claim that each soldier dies with dignity and meaning, in reality most soldiers die in obscurity, with no meaning behind their deaths other than bad luck. Every soldier's situation is almost as drastic as that of the soldiers whose bodies and dog tags are lost forever—their sacrifices are anonymous and quickly forgotten.

CHAPTERS 20–23

SUMMARY: CHAPTER 20

> *I also knew when I got back, she would expect me to*
> *be the same person, but it could never happen.*
>
> (See QUOTATIONS, p. 49)

During the evacuation, a scuffle breaks out between the Americans and their Vietnamese allies. The Vietnamese want to be evacuated first, so they threateningly surround the American troops. The American choppers, however, notice what is taking place and open fire on the Vietnamese, enabling the Americans to evacuate. Later, back at camp, Monaco suffers terrifying, vivid flashbacks. The squad celebrates what would have been Brew's nineteenth birthday.

Gearhart writes three copies of a letter to his wife and gives Richie and Walowick each a copy, in case something happens to Gearhart before he can mail his own copy. The letter is an average letter home, but Gearhart asks his wife to tell their children that he loves them. Richie thinks about how deeply he wishes that he had a wife and kids waiting for him at home—someone to connect him with life outside of war, someone who could make him look forward to returning to civilian life.

Richie finally writes a letter to Kenny about the realities of war, dispelling the war-movie myths of heroism and the idea that a stark division always exists between the good side and the bad side. He tells his brother that war is simply about killing the enemy before the enemy kills you. Right and wrong, Richie explains, are concepts that can only be contemplated in safety, far from the heat of battle. After writing the letter, he wonders how he will feel about his role in the war once he is back home and being hailed as a hero by his fellow countrymen.

SUMMARY: CHAPTER 21

Gearhart approaches the squad members and asks whether they would like to be broken up so that all the squads in the platoon are roughly equal in size. Staying together, he warns, would ensure that they are sent on missions more frequently than the other, more depleted squads. Despite the added danger, the squad refuses to split up. Richie and his friends now realize that the war is not going to end anytime soon and that the rumors of a coming truce have stopped circulating. Richie is unsure how much longer he can last, as his time in the hospital has severely softened him.

The squad is sent to patrol a nearby river where Vietcong activity is suspected. Though Brunner is the highest-ranking soldier among them, it quickly becomes clear that Johnson, with his quiet good sense, is the squad's true leader. The river seems quiet at first, with no enemies in sight. The squad then spots enemy soldiers hiding in the water among the reeds. Afraid that there are many more Vietcong present than initially suspected, the soldiers turn around to retreat. Richie and Peewee are sent across the river to secure a ridge on the way to the evacuation site. As they cross, they hear a firefight break out behind them.

SUMMARY: CHAPTER 22
Richie and Peewee become separated from their squad during the confusion and spend the night hiding in a small hole. Peeking out, they realize that an entire battalion of North Vietnamese has been patrolling the river. When an enemy soldier checks the hole in the morning, Richie and Peewee kill him and carefully make their way to the original chopper landing site, hoping that choppers will be sent there to look for them. At the landing zone, they find Monaco sitting alone, looking terrified. They quickly realize that there are enemy soldiers hiding in the bushes surrounding Monaco. The enemy soldiers are hoping to use Monaco as bait to draw in the choppers, and then kill Monaco along with all the Americans who land. When the chopper arrives, however, Peewee and Richie open fire on the enemy soldiers, alerting the choppers to the enemy presence and saving the lives of Monaco and many others. The choppers open fire on the Vietnamese, enabling all the Americans to board safely. Both Richie and Peewee are wounded during the scuffle.

SUMMARY: CHAPTER 23
Richie, Peewee, and Monaco are transported to a hospital. Monaco explains that he missed his evacuation from the area the night before because he lost consciousness during the struggle. Everyone else in the squad was evacuated safely. The doctors judge that Peewee is wounded seriously enough to return home, and Richie's medical profile is finally processed. Richie and Peewee are scheduled to return home on the same plane. Monaco receives orders to return to his unit. Upon his return to the front, he leaves a note for Richie, teasingly reminding him that he has to wear a tuxedo to the wedding.

Gearhart calls the hospital to report that the squad is doing well and that Stewart has finally received his promotion. Richie learns that Judy Duncan, however, was killed when her field hospital was bombed. While waiting for their flight home, Peewee and Richie read about the war in the newspapers and are struck by the fact that the stories give no sense of the true costs of the war. The papers report when a hill or village is secured, but do not mention the number of lives lost or the horror and confusion of the battle.

Richie and Peewee finally board the plane home, where they are surrounded by new soldiers just arriving in Vietnam and the caskets of dead soldiers. They hold hands the whole way home and try to adjust to the idea of returning to normal life, where petty concerns are the norm. The realization that he is actually returning to normal life finally hits Richie fully when he hears a fellow passenger complaining about the wine selection on the flight.

___

ANALYSIS: CHAPTERS 20–23

These final chapters mark the completion of Richie's development from an innocent youth in Harlem to a soldier who has witnessed violence, death, and fear. After Richie sees the carnage during the last mission with the full company—the burned corpses of his comrades, the lost dog tags, the mutilated civilians—he forces himself to write a candid letter to Kenny. He explains to his brother that he has killed out of fear and a desire to prevent the enemy from killing him first. He does not feel like a hero for what he does, since he wants merely to survive the war. In part, Richie is writing because the war has profoundly changed him in a matter of months, and he is trying to prepare his brother for this change. Like other soldiers, Richie will need his family's help if he wants to return to civilian life, and this reintroduction will require that those around him know the truth of his war experiences. Yet Richie also writes to Kenny out of a sense of obligation to correct the myths about war. Although these popular myths shield Richie's family members from doubt and fear, he does not want to lie to them any more. His drive to create a truthful portrait of life in combat suggests that he is becoming a man as well as a more successful writer. He is not content to spout comfortable clichés, but feels the need to present the truth, even if it is ugly.

The final chapters also highlight the tragic cycle of the war: boys ship into Vietnam full of life and brimming with ideals, only to ship out lifeless. The physical juxtaposition of the new recruits and the caskets of the dead soldiers foreshadows the inevitable annihilation these boys will suffer. Peewee and Richie are among the lucky ones, returning with their lives and bodies intact. Nonetheless, they have lost their innocence, their sense of normalcy and morality, their hope, and their faith. Richie and Peewee are returning home to a world that does not want to hear their real story, a world that simultaneously hates them for taking part in an unjust war and yearns to hold them up as valiant heroes. They are returning to a world that does not—and does not want to—understand them. They too are part of the life cycle, victims of a country that turns vibrant boys into corpses or depleted ghosts of their former selves.

The novel's tone during Richie and Peewee's return home is striking. Neither boy is jubilant, excited, or even happy. Rather, they are both numb and even frightened. Each knows that returning home will require almost as much strength as surviving in Vietnam. They will need to learn all over again how to live without the constant, foreboding sense of death. They will need to grapple with all the horrors they witnessed in Vietnam, and will need to reconnect with loved ones who cannot relate to what the soldiers have seen and experienced. Their loved ones will likely not understand the new people their experiences have caused them to become. Perhaps most difficult, they will have to reenter a world where petty concerns are treated with the same gravity as issues of life and death. The man on the plane who complains about the wine selection symbolizes this frivolity back home, a frivolity that Peewee and Richie once enjoyed.

IMPORTANT QUOTATIONS EXPLAINED

1. My plans, maybe just my dreams really, had been to go to college, and to write. . . . All the other guys in the neighborhood thought I was going to college. I wasn't, and the army was the place I was going to get away from all the questions.

In this passage from Chapter 2, Richie reflects on his dreams, giving us insight into his motivations for joining the army. Enlisting, we learn, was not a well-thought-out decision, but rather a form of escapism. Richie wanted to dodge the real world, questions about his future, and the frustration of seeing his hopes fizzle. He also hints that enlisting was an attempt to escape the judgment of others. He feels that those who had high expectations for him would be disappointed if he could not fulfill them.

Richie is also afraid of not living up to his dreams and disappointing himself. His inability to go to college and become a writer is not due to any personal failure—he excelled in high school—but simply to his family's extreme poverty. His father abandoned the family years ago, and his mother is a depressive alcoholic who wastes her money on liquor. Richie first calls his hopes for the future "plans" and then revises the word to "dreams," indicating that these were never really practical or even possible. These plans are impossible in part because of his impoverished situation but also in part because of the lack of encouragement from his mother, teachers, and guidance counselors, none of whom ever took his hopes seriously. As a result, Richie feels strong doubts about his future, which drive him to risk this future by enlisting in the army.

2. "My father used to call all soldiers angel warriors," he said. "Because usually they get boys to fight wars. Most of you aren't old enough to vote yet."

Lieutenant Carroll speaks these words following Jenkins's death in Chapter 4. His statement emphasizes one of the most important aspects of the novel: the extreme youth of the soldiers. Carroll's reference to the voting age highlights the tragic irony of the military: the fact that the people defending America are not old enough to have any say in the way the country is run and likely not mature enough to understand what they are fighting for. The irony only deepens when we remember that Carroll himself—who is seen as the wise, older leader—is only twenty-three years old. Carroll's reference to soldiers as "angel warriors" gives the novel its title, *Fallen Angels,* and suggests the innocence and naïveté of these young male soldiers. The statement also highlights Carroll's kindness and sensitivity, two of the traits that make him such a beloved commander and a good role model and leader. Unlike many other officers, such as Captain Stewart, Carroll is deeply affected by every death he sees. He does not try to increase the enemy body count to raise his chances of promotion. His only aim in Vietnam is to keep as many of his men alive as possible. It is his death—which occurs several weeks after he makes this statement—that shakes the squad irreparably.

QUOTATIONS

3.   We were supposed to smile a lot and treat the people
      with dignity. They were supposed to think we were the
      good guys. That bothered me a little. I didn't like
      having to convince anybody that I was the good
      guy. . . . We, the Americans, were the good guys.

Richie expresses these sentiments in Chapter 9, when he is unsettled
by the implications of his squad's pacification mission to a Vietnamese village. This statement reflects Richie's uncertainty about the
morality of the war; he is alarmed by the idea that the American
army would even have to convince the South Vietnamese that they
are the "good guys," because it reveals that their goodness is not an
obvious or unquestionable fact. Additionally, as the South Vietnamese are not necessarily happy to receive American assistance, the
Americans have to convince the South Vietnamese that an American
presence makes them better off.

Richie dislikes these questions about the ethics of the American
involvement in the Vietnam War because they challenge the comfortable, heroic, and romantic idea that he is fighting on the side of
right, acting as a hero to thousands of poor villagers. Richie's realization of the ambiguous morality of the war is the final—and most
damaging—blow to his adherence to the popular mythology of war.
Throughout his time in Vietnam, he comes to numerous painful
conclusions that change his worldview. He first recognizes that the
army is inefficient, fallible, and sometimes dishonest. He then realizes that war is irrational and chaotic and that living or dying is a
matter of luck. Later, he accepts that the war is not going to end anytime soon. Finally, he realizes that there is no clear distinction
between good and bad in the heat of combat, which causes him to
reevaluate his entire understanding of war and life.

4. We spent another day lying around. It seemed to be what the war was about. Hours of boredom, seconds of terror.

This statement, from Chapter 11, sums up the experience of life in Vietnam for many of the young men fighting there. While missions are terrifying, they are short bursts of horror and violence that last only hours or minutes. Even within missions, the squad spends much of the time waiting for something to happen. The stifling days or weeks between missions are in some ways even worse than the missions themselves, as soldiers are overcome with boredom, plagued by anxiety about the next mission, and tortured by memories of past horrors. It is during these downtimes when the soldiers in the squad tend to be pushed to their emotional limits. In fact, as Richie later admits, the missions bring along with them a level of excitement that sometimes overpowers the fear; any anxieties about the future and memories of the past fade, and the soldier lives in the pure present, acutely attuned to his body and everything around him. With just a few words, Myers conveys this strange timescale—hours or days of boredom, marked intermittently by seconds or minutes of terror—giving us a startling sense of what it is like to be a soldier in the middle of the Vietnam War.

QUOTATIONS

5.   I knew Mama loved me, but I also knew when I got back, she would expect me to be the same person, but it could never happen. She hadn't been to Nam. She hadn't given her poncho to anybody to wrap a body in, or stepped over a dying kid.

Richie expresses these sentiments in Chapter 20 after he reads Gearhart's letter to his wife. As Gearhart attempts to prepare his wife for his possible death, Richie begins to wish that he had a wife and children waiting for him at home. Throughout his tour of duty in Vietnam, Richie has longed to communicate successfully to someone back home about what the war is really like and what the war has done to him. His desire stems in part from a need to know that he will find someone understanding and sympathetic waiting for him if he returns alive. The desire also stems from a need to know that if he dies, someone back home will understand why and in what circumstances he died. Initially, Richie's desire manifests itself as a wish for a girlfriend, as he imagines that a girlfriend might be the sort of person who could truly understand what he has to tell. Now, he grabs on to the idea of a wife and children instead, thinking that perhaps they would be even better suited to try to understand what he has seen and who he has become. However, the only civilians with whom Richie can really communicate are his mother and Kenny, and he spends a large portion of his time in Vietnam contemplating ways to present the candid truth in a letter to them.

Key Facts

FULL TITLE
Fallen Angels

AUTHOR
Walter Dean Myers

TYPE OF WORK
Novel

GENRE
Coming-of-age story; historical fiction; war fiction

LANGUAGE
English

TIME AND PLACE WRITTEN
1988; Jersey City, New Jersey.

DATE OF FIRST PUBLICATION
1988

PUBLISHER
Scholastic Inc.

NARRATOR
Richie Perry, a young African-American soldier in the
Vietnam War

POINT OF VIEW
Richie tells the story in the first person, giving us
immediate, intimate access to his thoughts and feelings as the
action unfolds.

TONE
Richie speaks with immediacy and poignancy, baring his
innermost fears and thoughts. He filters the action of the novel
through the medium of these emotions and ideas.

TENSE
Past

SETTING (TIME)
Several months in 1967 and 1968

SETTING (PLACE)
Vietnam

PROTAGONIST
Richie Perry

MAJOR CONFLICT
Richie struggles to come to terms with the grim reality of war, which contradicts the myths about war that he believed going into it.

RISING ACTION
Richie's enlistment in the army to escape a bleak future; the misplacement of Richie's medical file, and his resulting assignment to Vietnam; Richie's burgeoning friendship with Peewee, Jenkins, and Johnson; the soldiers' journey to their camp near Chu Lai.

CLIMAX
Richie's success in drafting a truthful letter to his brother that discusses honestly the unromantic and gruesome nature of combat.

FALLING ACTION
The poorly planned mission on which the squad is sent; Peewee and Richie's separation from the rest of the squad; Peewee and Richie's quick thinking to save the lives of Monaco and the rest of the squad; Peewee's and Richie's getting wounded in the battle.

THEMES
The loss of innocence; the unromantic reality of war; the moral ambiguity of war

MOTIFS
Race; friendship; heroism

SYMBOLS
Richie's letters home; the lost dog tags; war movies

FORESHADOWING
The army's failure to process Richie's medical file properly hints that Richie will not receive a medical discharge and will have to fight; the army's bureaucratic mix-up at the airport in Osaka previews the general chaos of war and the ineffectiveness of trying to control that chaos.

STUDY QUESTIONS & ESSAY TOPICS

STUDY QUESTIONS

1. *How do Richie's beliefs about war change throughout his tour of duty in Vietnam?*

Richie joins the army with illusions and myths about war. He learned about war from movies and stories that portray battle as heroic and glorious, the army as efficient and organized, and warfare as rational. In these movies, the good, skillful people emerge victorious, while the bad people die. What Richie and the soldiers find in Vietnam bears no resemblance to this mythologized version of war. The army is inefficient and fallible. The bureaucracy fails to process Richie's medical profile for his injured knee, so he gets sent out to combat. Most of the officers who command Richie and his peers are far from heroic—looking out for their own lives at best and their own careers at worst. There are a few noble exceptions, such as Lieutenant Carroll—men who risk their own lives to save the men under them. In the heat of battle, soldiers think of nothing but self-preservation. Paralyzed by fear, they act thoughtlessly, often killing their allies in the process. Battles are far from organized and are instead utterly chaotic. The Vietnamese villagers are not happy to receive help from the Americans, and the Vietcong often kill such villagers for accepting supplies from the American forces.

At the beginning of his tour of duty, Richie clings to the myth that people die only if they are not smart and careful, but he realizes that in battle, life or death is just a matter of chance. There is no way to be smart or careful during such a war. The political ideology behind the war turns out to be similarly unrealistic. Richie is first inspired to think of fighting for his country and for ideals like freedom and democracy, but in the heat of battle, such rhetoric becomes empty. As the men are surrounded by the horrors of war, the neat divisions between right and wrong fade, and the sense of being on the side of good is no longer as easy to maintain. Rather than fight for country or freedom, Richie realizes that the soldiers fight to stay alive.

2.   *How do war movies perpetuate the romantic ideals of war? How does* Fallen Angels *criticize these movies and myths?*

War movies exhibit the clichés of war myths common in American popular culture, such as the inevitable tragic death of any baby-faced virgin soldier. The presence of such stories about war is chilling because it reveals a tendency to romanticize real wartime trage-dies. Such clichés attach false meaning to deaths that are often senseless and brutal, not beautiful and romantic like the customary myths. In many cases, American soldiers die, and terror makes other American soldiers careless. When Richie patrols with another com-pany, for instance, one American platoon mistakes another Ameri-can platoon for the enemy and kills more than a dozen friendly soldiers before realizing the mistake.

The romanticized myths of the soldier's heroism and patriotism may help a soldier's family deal with his death because it gives the parents a reason for the sacrifice of their son. However, these myths do not allow civilians to acknowledge the brutality and ugliness that American sons must face when they go to war. These myths do not do justice to the soldiers' sacrifices. They also make it difficult for the soldier to share his burden of fear and suffering with his family. Richie is unable to tell his mother and Kenny the truth about the war because he does not want to upset them or lower their opinions of him. He does not want them to feel the fear and anxiety that he feels during his time in Vietnam.

3.   *How do the soldiers cope with the horrors that they see?*
     Contrast the coping mechanisms of Richie, Peewee,
     and Lobel.

Faced with the horrors of war, each soldier must either reconcile reality with his personal beliefs or cling tenaciously to comfortable illusions of absolute morality. Richie, unlike many of the other soldiers, chooses the difficult first option, struggling to make sense of his experiences and refusing to turn away from the difficult questions they raise. Richie's comrades, who are too afraid to come to terms with the reality of their situation, warn him against what they call his dangerous thinking. Each soldier has his own way of blocking out the uncomfortable thoughts and nagging doubts. Richie recognizes that he is alone in his search for truth, reflecting that "the questions kept coming and nobody wanted to deal with them." Yet just as his friends cannot bear to look the reality head on, Richie cannot bear to ignore it.

Peewee and Lobel both try to understand their role in the war, but do so in different ways because of their different personalities and backgrounds. Peewee responds to fear and confusion with brash humor, making jokes out of any unsettling doubts. When Peewee is momentarily stunned by the Vietnamese mother's sacrifice of her child, Richie is able to pull himself out of his paralysis by joking, "They got kids over here?" Moments later he casually asks, "Me? Feel bad? . . . Never happen," showing that he hides his emotions behind a facade of bravado. Lobel, on the other hand, turns to movies as his escape. He views Vietnam as a giant movie set and sees himself as the star of a war film. His obsession with movies is more than a simple diversion—it is an escape from a reality that is too difficult for Lobel to face unprotected. He desperately clings to the belief that the movies are "the only real thing in life," thereby allowing himself to dismiss the horrible sights he sees around him as unreal. Like Peewee's humor, Lobel's obsession with movies helps him filter out the tough questions of morality that plague Richie. By believing that the world of movies is more real than the battlefield, Lobel can pretend that such difficult questions are not even worth asking.

SUGGESTED ESSAY TOPICS

1. Compare *Fallen Angels* to *All Quiet on the Western Front,* Erich Maria Remarque's famous antiwar novel from World War I. What themes do these novels have in common? How are they different? Would you characterize *Fallen Angels* as an antiwar novel? Why or why not?

2. How does *Fallen Angels* address matters of race and class in America? How does the novel portray the effects of the war on race and class issues, and the effects of race and class issues on the war? Why is it ironic that so many war protesters are college students?

3. Trace Richie's attitude toward the war through his letters to his family. What is the significance of his longtime inability to write an honest letter? What is the significance of his eventual ability to write a truthful letter to Kenny?

4. Explain the different styles of leadership of Captain Stewart, Sergeant Simpson, Lieutenant Carroll, Lieutenant Gearhart, Corporal Brunner, and Sergeant Dongan. What is the novel's attitude toward each of their styles?

QUESTIONS & ESSAYS

REVIEW & RESOURCES

QUIZ

1. Which of the following leads Richie to enlist in the army?

   A. He thinks the army will be fun and adventurous
   B. He is unsure what to make of his future and too poor to afford to go to college
   C. He is interested in a military career
   D. None of the above

2. Why does Earlene end her relationship with Peewee?

   A. She is against the war effort and does not want to date a soldier
   B. He does not write her enough letters
   C. Her parents have forbidden her to have a relationship with a soldier
   D. She is marrying someone else

3. What are the circumstances of Jenkins's death?

   A. He dies senselessly after he accidentally steps on a land mine
   B. He dies a meaningful death because he sacrifices his life to save other soldiers
   C. He dies during an important, crucial mission to secure a village
   D. None of the above

4. How does Lobel cope with his fear?

   A. He drinks
   B. He thinks of the war as a movie in which he plays the part of the soldier who never dies
   C. He projects an image of toughness with false bravado
   D. None of the above

5. How does Peewee cope with his fear?

    A. He sleeps with the village women
    B. He views the war as a battle to protect democratic ideals
    C. Through bravado and humor
    D. None of the above

6. Besides combat, what problems do Richie and his fellow soldiers face?

    A. Life-threatening diseases
    B. The petty careerism of their commanding officers
    C. Racist commanding officers
    D. All of the above

7. Why does Richie not tell his mother or brother the truth about his war experiences?

    A. He wants to shield them from fear and anxiety
    B. He does not want to lower their opinion of him
    C. He does not know what to think about the war himself
    D. All of the above

8. Which of the following best describes Richie's letter to Lieutenant Carroll's wife about Carroll's death?

    A. The letter describes the reality of Carroll's death because Richie believes that Carroll's wife deserves the truth
    B. The letter reveals Richie's grief and shock at Carroll's death
    C. The letter is polite but impersonal
    D. None of the above

9. What did Richie dream of doing before he enlisted in the army?

    A. Going to college and becoming a writer
    B. Opening his own business
    C. Becoming a basketball player
    D. Becoming a teacher

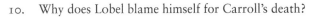

10. Why does Lobel blame himself for Carroll's death?

    A. He thinks that he accidentally exposed Carroll's position to the Vietcong

    B. He thinks that he was so paralyzed by fear that he was unable to fire his gun during the mission

    C. He thinks that Carroll died while trying to save his life

    D. He thinks that his gun misfired and accidentally hit Carroll

11. What happens when Lieutenant Gearhart goes on his first patrol mission?

    A. Everything goes smoothly because of Gearhart's good judgment and extensive combat experience

    B. Gearhart's platoon mistakes another platoon for the enemy and kills more than a dozen American soldiers before realizing the mistake

    C. Jenkins, a new soldier, steps on a land mine and dies

    D. Gearhart accidentally sets off a flare and reveals his soldiers' position to the enemy

12. What is most important to Captain Stewart?

    A. Ensuring that the men under his command are treated fairly

    B. Earning a promotion

    C. Surviving until the end of his tour of duty

    D. Winning the war

13. What is most important to Sergeant Simpson?

    A. Surviving until the end of his tour of duty

    B. Winning the war

    C. Earning a promotion

    D. Ensuring that the men under his command are treated fairly

14. Why does Lobel enlist in the army?

   A. He feels that it is his patriotic duty
   B. He wants to convince his father that he is not a homosexual
   C. His father is a colonel, so he wants to follow the family tradition
   D. He wants to stop the spread of Communism

15. Which of the following best describes the relationship between Richie and his mother prior to the war?

   A. They have a close, harmonious relationship
   B. They are not very close, but they generally get along with each other
   C. They are close, but they frequently clash with each other
   D. They are not very close, and they have frequent disagreements with each other

16. How does the war change the relationship between Richie and his mother?

   A. It makes it worse because Richie's mother is against the war
   B. It makes it better because Richie's mother is a firm supporter of the war
   C. It makes it better because it makes them realize how much they need each other
   D. None of the above

17. How does Richie injure his knee?

   A. Playing basketball in basic training
   B. He is shot in the knee during a combat mission
   C. Playing baseball in basic training
   D. Fighting another student in high school

18. How does Lobel's father feel about the war?

    A.   He is a firm supporter of the war

    B.   He is against the war

    C.   He does not have a firm opinion about the war, but he thinks Lobel is foolish and reckless to enlist in the army

    D.   None of the above

19. How many Purple Hearts does Richie earn in the war?

    A.   Two

    B.   One

    C.   Three

    D.   None of the above

20. How do Johnson and Walowick cope with having to kill people in the war?

    A.   They tell themselves that they are doing their patriotic duty

    B.   They drink a lot

    C.   They understand that they have to kill or be killed

    D.   They tell themselves that the enemy soldiers are the bad guys

21. Which of the following men do Peewee and Richie save from certain death?

    A.   Johnson

    B.   Monaco

    C.   Walowick

    D.   Simpson

22. Which of the following men is devoutly religious?

    A.   Johnson

    B.   Peewee

    C.   Brew

    D.   Walowick

23. How does Richie feel about being ordered to return to his unit after he recuperates from his first wound?

   A. He is terrified and briefly considers going AWOL
   B. He is eager to return to battle
   C. He is not happy about having to return to combat, but decides that he will work hard for a promotion
   D. He is happy to fulfill his patriotic duty

24. How does Richie's father feel about the war?

   A. He is against the war
   B. He is a firm supporter of the war
   C. He is ambivalent about the war
   D. We do not know because Richie's father abandoned the family years ago

25. Why does Richie finally leave Vietnam at the end of *Fallen Angels*?

   A. He receives a wound that is serious enough to merit a discharge
   B. His medical profile is finally processed
   C. He has served his full tour of duty
   D. His mother dies and he must take care of Kenny

Suggestions for Further Reading

DENENBERG, BARRY. *Voices from Vietnam.* New York: Scholastic, 1997.

DREW, BERNARD A. *The 100 Most Popular Young Adult Authors: Biographical Sketches and Bibliographies.* Greenwood Village, Colorado: Libraries Unlimited, 1997.

EDELMAN, BERNARD. *Dear America: Letters Home from Vietnam.* New York: Norton, 1985.

O'BRIEN, TIM. *The Things They Carried.* Boston: Houghton Mifflin, 1990.

SUTTON, ROGER. *Threads in Our Cultural Fabric: A Conversation with Walter Dean Myers.* School Library Journal, v40. 24–28, June 1994.

REVIEW & RESOURCES

A Note on the Type

The typeface used in SparkNotes study guides is Sabon, created by master typographer Jan Tschichold in 1964. Tschichold revolutionized the field of graphic design twice: first with his use of asymmetrical layouts and sanserif type in the 1930s when he was affiliated with the Bauhaus, then by abandoning assymetry and calling for a return to the classic ideals of design. Sabon, his only extant typeface, is emblematic of his latter program: Tschichold's design is a recreation of the types made by Claude Garamond, the great French typographer of the Renaissance, and his contemporary Robert Granjon. Fittingly, it is named for Garamond's apprentice, Jacques Sabon.

SparkNotes
Test Preparation
Guides

The SparkNotes team figured it was time to cut standardized tests
down to size. We've studied the tests for you, so that SparkNotes
test prep guides are:

Smarter:
Packed with critical-thinking skills and test-
    taking strategies that will improve your score.

Better:
Fully up to date, covering all new features of the tests,
    with study tips on every type of question.

Faster:
Our books cover exactly what you need to
    know for the test. No more, no less.

SparkNotes Study Guides: